mjf

happiness

it's never too late...

patrick lindsay

MJF BOOKS
NEW YORK

Published by MJF Books
Fine Communications
322 Eighth Avenue
New York, NY 10001

happiness: it's never too late...
Text copyright © 2002 Patrick Lindsay
LC Control Number 2006907780
ISBN-13: 978-1-56731-848-7
ISBN-10: 1-56731-848-7

Originally published by Hardie Grant Books.
This edition published by MJF Books in arrangement with Lime Tree Productions.

Artworks copyright © Angela Brennan. Frontispiece: In the world or on earth, 1998; Page 7: Untitled; Pages 14–15: Take me there (2), 2004; Page 22: Saying, 2003; Page 29: Exile and the kingdom (2), 2004; Pages 36–37: Elegant and beautiful, 1992; Page 42: Mint blankets and love lawns (2), 1998; Jacket and page 47: Orange circles, 2003; Pages 54–55: My, 2003; Page 62: Song painting, c. 1995; Page 69: China Mary, 2002; Pages 76–77: 29 desires and 3 beliefs, 2002; Page 84: Checks, 2002; Page 91: Many, almost one, 1997; Page 98: Checks, 2004; Page 105: Freedom and necessity, 1995.

Design and typesetting by Kate Mitchell Design.

Printed in Singapore.

MJF Books and the MJF colophon are trademarks of Fine Creative Media, Inc.

TWP   10   9   8   7   6   5   4   3   2   1

to

Lisa, Nathan, Kate and Sarah

for

all those who want to be the best they can …
and have fun getting there.

Follow your heart

First, know your heart.
It knows things your mind can't understand.
Listen to it.
Listen above the crowd.
Be open to it.
Let it guide you on the big decisions.
Be true to it.

The heart has its reasons, which reason knows nothing of.
Blaise Pascal

Be faithful

It sounds so old-fashioned.
But fidelity is the foundation of so many
valuable things.
Like love,
mateship
and family.
Most importantly, be faithful to yourself.
And your core beliefs.

Live your beliefs and you can turn the world around.
Henry David Thoreau

Accentuate the positive

Too often we dwell on the negatives.
This weighs us down.
Look for the upside.
See the light rather than the dark side.
Search for positive energy.
It will transform your attitude.
It will empower you.
And reignite your passion.

Keep sowing your seeds, for you never know
which one will grow – perhaps they all will.
The Bible

Explore a mystery

Take the challenge.
Back your judgement.
Draw on your experience.
Look with different eyes.
Ask questions.
Especially the obvious ones.
Go back to original sources.
Crosscheck them.
Begin to unravel it.

Be an opener of doors.
Ralph Waldo Emerson

4

Stop complaining

Grizzling achieves nothing.
Just stirs animosity.
Promotes negatives.
And excuses.
Look through others' eyes.
See the positives.
Seek solutions.
Make positive suggestions.
Help implement them.
You'll be surprised at your reception.

Never complain, never explain.
Benjamin Disraeli

Take the path least travelled

It takes courage and confidence.
It has some risks but it often brings great rewards:
the challenge of the new;
the thrill of exploration;
growth from the learning;
and self-confidence from success.

We know what happens to people who stay in
the middle of the road, they get run over.
Aneurin Bevan

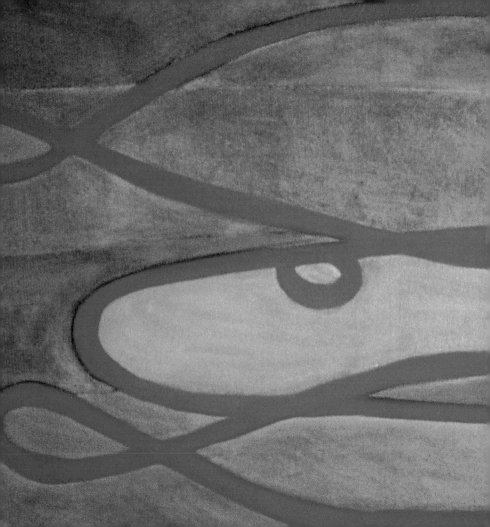

Remember people's names

It seems such a small thing to you.
But it's so important to others.
And so memorable.
When you're introduced, greet people by name.
Make a mental note.
Associate the name with the face.
If you take the trouble to remember someone's name,
they'll remember you.
And hold you in high regard.

A man dies and leaves a name; a tiger dies and leaves a skin.
Chinese saying

Be patient

With experience we realise the importance of patience.
Too many decisions are reflex actions.
Take the time to ponder.
Put things in perspective.
Allow situations to develop.
Sense the patterns of things.
Wait until the moment is right.
Then be decisive.

Can you remain unmoving until the right action arises by itself?
Tao Te Ching

Be honest with yourself

We can fool others.
But we can't fool ourselves.
Being honest with yourself brings freedom.
Work towards self-acceptance.
Respect yourself as you would want
others to respect you.
Find your truths.
Aspire to be a better person.

An honest man is the noblest work of God.
Alexander Pope

Enjoy the trip

No matter how far you travel.
Or how long the trip.
Across the city.
Across the country.
Across the world.
Or through your life.
The journey matters more than the destination.
Enjoy the journey.

Every journey starts with the first step.
Chinese proverb

It's never too late to . . .

Do your best

How often we say it.
How often we promise to do it.
Yet how rarely do we actually do the best we can.
When we do –
when we use all our efforts,
when we push through old boundaries –
the satisfaction is enormous.
And the rewards are sweeter because
they've been earned.

Make the most of yourself, for that is all there is of you.
Ralph Waldo Emerson

Return your calls

It's so easy to ignore messages.
Sometimes it's justified.
But put yourself in their shoes.
There's nothing worse than being ignored.
You're bigger than that.
Give a little of yourself.
Give them the courtesy you'd hope to receive.
Whether they're phone calls or calls for help,
answer them.
In the long-term you'll be the winner.

There are only the pursued, the pursuing, the busy and the tired.
F. Scott Fitzgerald

Help the earth

We're only borrowing the earth while we're here.
We must hand it on to the next generation.
Let's do what we can to improve it.
Or at least do as little damage as possible.
Do the simple things.
Recycle.
Join in community clean-ups.
Try solar energy.
Walk, cycle, car-pool, catch a bus.
Watch over our oceans.
Protect the forests.

The world is a fine place and worth fighting for.
Ernest Hemingway

Free-fall

Most of our lives are structured.
Most of our actions planned.
Most of our risks covered.
All the more reason to free-fall sometimes.
Go with your instincts.
Let your heart lead.
Take a chance.

Freedom has a thousand charms to show.
That slaves, howe'er contented, never know.
William Cowper

Plan for the future

Set goals.
They give direction and purpose.
And a sense of optimism.
But paint with a broad brush.
Fill in the details as needed.
Plan for tomorrow.
But live a day at a time.

We never prepared any battle plan without at least one alternate plan.
General George S. Patton

Listen to the rain

Let it soothe your spirit.
Smell the freshness.
Hear the patterns.
See the cleansing.
The way trees and plants drink it in.
Feel the renewal.

The sound of the rain is like the voices of
tens of thousands of monks reading sutras.
Yukio Mishima

Walk through the bush

Feel the power in your legs.
The strength in your lungs.
Soak up the sounds of the birds,
and the wind.
Enjoy the scents,
and the colours of the season.
Observe the cycles of birth and growth,
death and regrowth.

Your house shall not be an anchor but a mast.
Kahlil Gibran

Skinny-dip in the sea

Be bold.
Let the ocean carry you,
and caress you.
Feel its endless rhythm,
and power.
Let the salt water heal you.
Explore its depths.
Adopt its freedom.

I have bathed in the Poem of the Sea ...
Arthur Rimbaud

Walk barefoot

Feel the sand between your toes,
and the living grass.
The warmth of the sun on the road.
Connect with the earth.
Feel the different textures.
Enliven your senses.
Savour the freedom.

Adopt the pace of nature: her secret is patience.
Ralph Waldo Emerson

Change direction

Even a small change can reap big benefits.
Consider alternatives.
Look with fresh eyes.
Register patterns.
Feel where you are blocked or stale.
Try something new.
Start with small things and experience the difference.
Then you'll see the more important changes …
and you'll make them naturally.

True life is lived when tiny changes occur.
Leo Tolstoy

Pause awhile

We all need time to reflect,
to put things in perspective.
To see the truly valuable things in our life,
and to appreciate them.
To reflect properly, we must be calm and balanced.
Put your life on pause.
Sit on a quiet beach,
or in a tranquil garden.
Somewhere you can muse without distraction.
Calmness and balance will join you there.

The hardest thing to see is what is in front of your eyes.
Johann Wolfgang von Goethe

Look at the big picture

Too often, life pushes in on us.
It narrows our vision.
Listen without filtering.
Observe without prejudice.
Allow things to wash over you and open your mind.
See things against the past.
Consider them in the light of the future.
Take an expansive view.

What lies behind us and what lies before us are tiny matters
compared to what lies within us.
Ralph Waldo Emerson

Enjoy the silence

In a world of constant clamour,
silence can be pure pleasure.
It can provide a haven.
And allow your own melodies to flourish.
Seek out the quiet corners.
Enjoy the liberating space they provide.
Fill the silent space with calm thoughts.
And revive your spirits.

Silence is golden.
Proverb

Make a comeback

Whatever the position,
whatever the expectations,
you're always in the game,
if you believe you're in the game.
You have the power.
With self-belief and determination, you can change
your fortunes.
You can turn things around.
You can come back.

Never give in. Never give in. Never give in.
Sir Winston Churchill

Ignore the pessimists

Avoid their company,
and their dark vibes.
They thrive on failure and negativity.
Rise above them.
Trust your instincts and your ability.
Set your own standards and goals.
Aim high.
Strive for great things.

The optimist proclaims that we live in the best of all possible worlds;
and the pessimist fears this is true.
James Branch Cabell

Stop being a victim

Take a hard look at yourself.
Are you a willing victim?
Do you take the line of least resistance?
Then blame others, or circumstances, or fate?
It's a matter of pride and self-respect,
and the respect of others.
Stand up for yourself, for your rights, for your beliefs.
Others will appreciate your efforts.
And, surprisingly, many will help you.

Life is either a daring adventure or nothing.
Helen Keller

Learn to surf

Few things bring greater harmony with nature.
Look with awe at nature's power.
Wonder at the rhythm of the waves and swells.
There is poetry here.
Find a teacher who appreciates the elegance of the art.
Then draw from the ocean's energy to find your place.

Life is rhythm. Life stops when the heart stops beating.
Angelique Kidjo

Stop underestimating yourself

Too often we take ourselves for granted.
Or worse, we only see our failures,
mistakes or imperfections.
Give yourself credit where it's due.
Look at the other side of the ledger.
Start appreciating your achievements.
Understand how you reached them.
Recall the satisfaction of a job well done.
Build on that feeling.
Seek to duplicate it.

Never desert your own line of talent.
Sydney Smith

Take a cryptic challenge

It's a mental Mount Everest to most of us.
But it's all in our mind-set.
Warm up with quick or simple puzzles.
Use a dictionary or thesaurus when you're stuck.
Take your time and gain confidence.
Step up to the cryptic challenge.
Look through the writer's eyes.
Learn the language of the game.
Persist until you see the patterns.
Then it will open for you.

With words we govern men.
Benjamin Disraeli

Take control of a computer

Refuse to be intimidated.
You don't have to know how the engine works …
just how to drive it.
Take time to explore the system.
Patience is crucial.
Move slowly at first so you can undo mistakes.
Build your skills.
Become the driver.

Victory belongs to the most persevering.
Napoleon Bonaparte

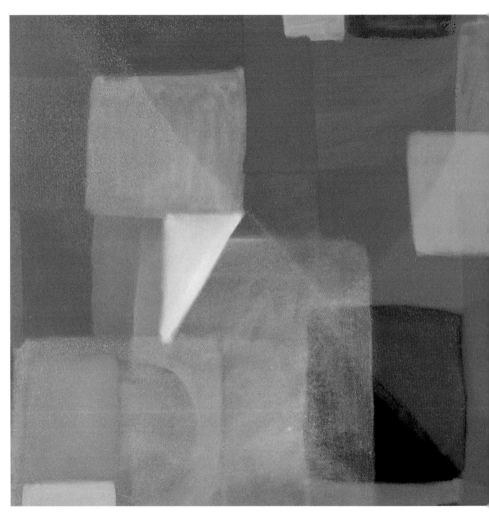

Plan for the future

It's vital to live in the present,
but sometimes take a wider view and look ahead.
Visualise your plans,
then file them away in the back of your mind.
Allow them to develop there.
They'll act as subconscious guideposts,
and quietly show you which paths
to take to achieve them.

Yesterday is but today's memory and tomorrow is today's dream.
Kahlil Gibran

Visit a friend

A surprise visit is a great gift to a friend.
It shows you've been thinking of them.
More than that, it shows how much
you value their friendship.
It will lift their spirits.
It will warm up your day.

We can do no great things – only small things with great love.
Katherine Mansfield

Go back to your roots

Rewind your life.
Spool through the memories.
Relive some of the highlights.
Recall some of the characters who travelled with you.
Revisit some of the places that helped form your views.
See how far you've travelled.
Discover the things that matter.
Cherish them.

To understand where you are going you must
understand where you come from.
Celtic proverb

Look in the mirror

Take a long look.
Peer deeply into your eyes.
Try to see behind the façade.
What kind of person are you?
Do you like what you see?
Do the good things outweigh the bad?
Work on yourself so that they do.

In youth we learn; in age we understand.
Marie Ebner-Eschenbach

Reward yourself

It's a question of balance.
Don't take it too far and become selfish,
but don't ignore yourself.
Be honest.
When you deserve it, reward yourself.
We all respond to positive reinforcement.

Self is a sea boundless and measureless.
Kahlil Gibran

Visualise your dream

This is a most underrated tool.
It's long been used in sport.
Use it in life.
Picture yourself achieving your goals.
Place yourself in the picture.
Think deeply on it,
and you'll be surprised how often your visualisation
becomes reality.

Live the life you've imagined.
Henry David Thoreau

Be ready

Opportunity often knocks on empty doors.
Hold yourself ready to achieve your goals.
If you can prepare yourself for success, do so.
If your dream requires training or homework, do it.
If it means letting people know what you want, do it.
Eliminate every barrier you can.
Give yourself every chance to get there.
And chances are you will.

I dream of things that never were and say 'why not?'
Robert Fitzgerald Kennedy

Push your luck

You've got to be in it to win it.
Give yourself the best chance you can.
Try your hand.
Be sensible but have a real go.
Pause and think:
if you don't try, will you regret it?
Go your hardest!

You miss one hundred per cent of the shots you don't take.
Wayne Gretzky

Learn to swim

Swimming opens another world,
one of beauty and grace.
Water is essential to life.
It is your friend.
Allow yourself to meld with it.
Feel it support you.
Move like a dolphin.
Embrace the solitude.

Swim with the tide.
Anonymous

Look for the inner beauty

We all have it.
Although some camouflage it very well.
And some hide it deep inside.
Take the time to search for it.
It's always there.
And the reward is worth the effort.

The most important things in life are not things.
Anonymous

Stand on your own two feet

You can't find real fulfilment unless you do.
You can't flourish in someone's shadow.
Take the risks.
Endure the falls.
Learn from them.
Enjoy the self-respect.
Savour the freedom.

The worst loneliness is not to be comfortable with yourself.
Mark Twain

Put the past behind you

You can't change it.
So don't wear it like a chain.
Understand it.
Learn from it.
Turn the experience into a positive.
Use it to look ahead.

I will go anywhere provided it be forward.
Dr David Livingstone

Find your artistic side

Every child has one.
As we grow up, many of us have it denied.
Or diminished.
Or constrained.
Or mocked.
But it's still there.
Look for it.
Discover it.
Release it.

One eye sees, the other feels.
Paul Klee

Learn something every day

Make it a golden rule.
Every day, open your mind to something new.
It can come from nature, from others or from within.
Be aware.
Question the mundane.
Allow new things into your consciousness.
Relish the challenge.

Everybody is ignorant, only on different subjects.
Will Rogers

Give credit

It brings reciprocal benefits to giver and receiver.
It liberates the giver
and renews the receiver's faith.
It transforms relationships
and forges trust.
It encourages greater effort.
It's the right thing to do.

Credit where credit is due.
Anonymous

Amaze yourself

We use such a small amount of our capacity.
We constantly err on the side of caution.
Take the leap.
Extend yourself.
Move out of your comfort zone.
It's worth the risk.

Boldness has genius, power and magic in it.
Johann Wolfgang von Goethe

Honour a veteran

We owe them so much.
Our freedom.
Our future.
They rarely ask for anything.
The least they deserve is recognition for their sacrifices.
A simple thank you will mean much to them.
Ask them about their personal stories.
And you will be richly rewarded.

Old soldiers never die; they just fade away.
General Douglas MacArthur

Do the right thing

It sounds so obvious.
Our inner compass is rarely wrong.
But we often ignore it.
Or avoid it.
Take notice of it.
Act on your feeling.
The satisfaction is well worth it.

Perfect kindness acts without thinking of kindness.
Lao-Tzu

Rise to the occasion

Most of us live quietly on the fringes.
We're content to let others take centre stage.
But there will come a time when you'll face a choice:
stay in the shadows or stride into the light.
You'll know when the time is right.
Take your chance.
Make it count.

When a decision has to be made, make it.
There is no totally right time for anything.
General George S. Patton

Astral travel

We all need a change of scenery at some time.
When you can't make a physical change …
do it in your mind.
Let your imagination run free.
Fly at will.
Visit your dream locations.
Explore the possibilities.

The real voyage of discovery consists not in seeking
new landscapes but in having new eyes.
Marcel Proust

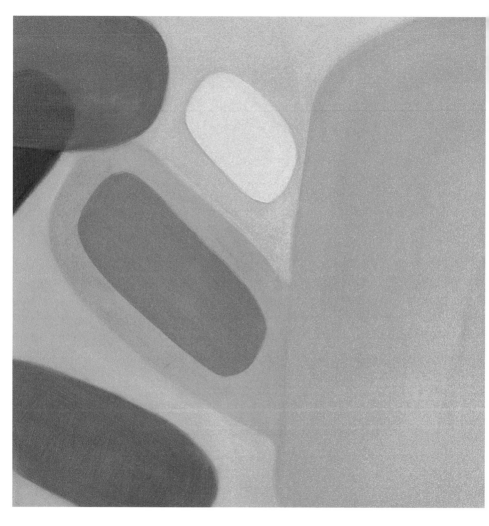

Avert a disaster

If you can foresee a problem, however big or small,
you must act.
Think through the consequences.
Consider the damage.
Find the courage to speak up.

Courage is only the accumulation of small steps.
George Konrad

Develop a backbone

If you've endured oppression.
If you've bowed to pressure.
If you've failed to fight back.
Stop being the doormat.
Look within.
Respect yourself.
Decide what's really important to you.
Draw your boundaries.
Fight for them.

You must do the thing you think you can't do.
Eleanor Roosevelt

Bare your soul

It can be wonderfully liberating,
but it's a gift to bestow with discernment.
The time and place must be right,
and, even more importantly, so must the person.
It takes courage to be vulnerable.
Feel the freedom.

The less you open your heart to others, the more your heart suffers.
Deepak Chopra

It's never too late to …

Bite your tongue

When your blood is boiling,
and every instinct is telling you to shout back,
hold your tongue.
It can often prevent damage to others.
Or save you regrets.
It can even give you an advantage,
as you maintain control.

If you are patient in one moment of anger,
you will avoid one hundred days of sorrow.
Chinese proverb

Blaze a trail

Many of us fear change,
but it can often liberate and revitalise.
It doesn't have to be big.
Take a different route to work.
Try a new dish.
Make new friends.
Learn a new language.
Breaking new ground brings great satisfaction.

Begin difficult things while they are easy.
Lao-Tzu

Break the cycle

When you're in a rut.
First, recognise the cycle in which you're trapped.
Then, consider ways to break out of it.
Most of our restrictions are imaginary.
Many disappear simply by viewing things differently.
Others need a different plan.
But, when you put your mind to it,
there's always a plan.

The attempt and not the deed confounds us.
William Shakespeare

Care

Too often we rush through life.
And people and things seem like props in a movie.
Take the time to look about you.
The important things will stand out.
These are the things to care about.

Is not love, even as time is, undivided and paceless?
Kahlil Gibran

Celebrate

Life is too short not to celebrate.
Too often we concentrate on our failures,
or the negatives we encounter.
Enjoy the successes.
Savour the victories, big or small.
Make them memorable and worthwhile,
and you're more likely to repeat them.

Laughter is wine for the soul.
Sean O'Casey

Channel your energies

Sometimes we have to be single-minded.
It's the only way to achieve some goals.
We have to draw on all our energy,
all our skills, all our determination.
When we do, there's very little we can't accomplish.

Concentration comes out of a combination of confidence and hunger.
Arnold Palmer

Clear the air

The longer we let problems fester,
the more damage they cause.
Confronting them always seems far worse
than it turns out to be.
Once you take the first step, most problems evaporate.
Deal with things.
Then you can get on with the journey,
and leave the baggage behind.

If you know the enemy and you know yourself,
you need not fear the result of a hundred battles.
Sun Tzu

Reach closure

Without closure, the wounds remain open,
the hurt continues,
the fear lingers.
Only by facing the fear,
righting the wrong,
saying farewell,
can we achieve peace of mind and move forward.

Forgiveness does not change the past, but it does enlarge the future.
Paul Boese

Confront your fears

So easy to say.
So difficult to do.
But, until you face your fears,
you're always looking back.
You're a diminished version of yourself.
Do it by degrees.
Do it with the help of others.
But stare down your fears.
Watch yourself grow as the fears shrink.

I'm never afraid of what I know.
Anna Sewell

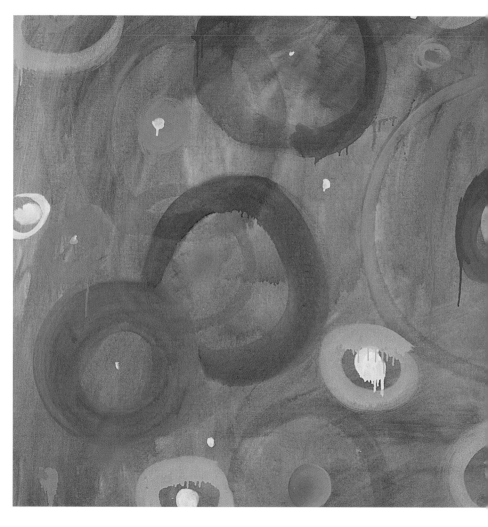

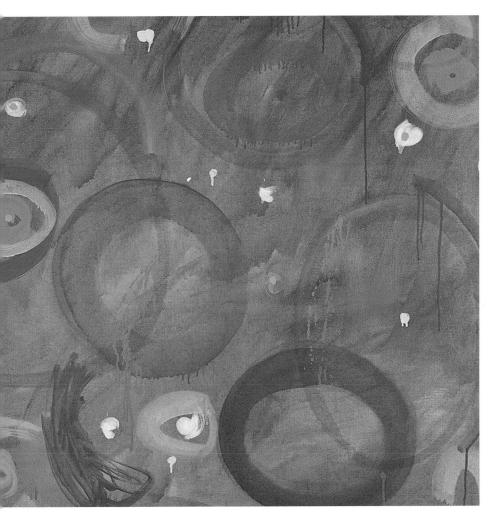

Cut your losses

Every good poker player knows it:
sometimes you have to throw in your hand.
The trick is knowing when to fight on,
and when to bail out.
A good general rule:
when it's causing more harm than good,
it's time to leave it.

Being able to persist is not the most important thing
– the ability to start over is.
F. Scott Fitzgerald

Have a massage

Never underestimate the power of touch.
It reassures and soothes,
relaxes and revitalises.
In expert hands, it nourishes and
restores body and spirit.
It brings great satisfaction to giver and receiver.

They reached out their hands in longing for the further shore.
Virgil

Delegate

It's one of the most valuable
– and most underused – skills.
It's not about avoiding responsibility.
It's a positive action.
Give someone the chance to be part of the team.
Allow the receiver to show initiative
and the giver to grow.

A leader is a man who can adapt principles to circumstances.
General George S. Patton

Deliver

So often we bail out before finishing the task.
We'll always find excuses to justify it,
but then we live in the shadow of unfulfilled promises.
Whenever you can, move out of these shadows.
No matter how long it takes,
whether big or small,
finish the job.
You'll be amazed at the freedom it brings.

Give us the tools and we will finish the job.
Sir Winston Churchill

Do your own thing

Everywhere, we're urged to conform.
To join the club.
To be like everyone else.
Resist that urge.
Look inside and discover the essential you.
Be true to yourself.
Follow your own path.

Don't compromise yourself. You're all you've got.
Janis Joplin

Emerge from the shadows

You don't have to grab the limelight,
but don't live in the shadow of others.
Claim your place under the sun.
You can do it on your own terms.
You don't have to push others aside.
For your dignity and self-esteem, stand your ground.
Watch how others' opinions of you rise.

Whether you think you will succeed or not – you're right.
Henry Ford

Lose the stress

It's holding you back.
It's stifling your creativity.
It may even be killing you.
Locate the stresses in your life:
isolate them;
challenge them.
Replace them with alternatives:
change, meditation, exercise.

A field that has rested gives a beautiful crop.
Ovid

Downshift

Discard some of that landfill we all accumulate.
Pare back unnecessary material baggage.
You'll discard a lot of mental and
spiritual baggage as well.
It will open real meaning in your life.
You'll view things with renewed clarity.
You'll step off on new paths.

Think simple. Reduce the whole of its parts into the simplest terms,
getting back to first principles.
Frank Lloyd Wright

Make the call yourself

Too often we allow others to choose our path.
That's usually the line of least resistance.
It provides a built-in excuse should things go awry.
But it also brings the least satisfaction.
Take the responsibility.
Shoulder the risks.
Explore the possibilities.
Make the call.
Enjoy the rewards.

A man who makes no mistakes does not usually make anything.
Edward John Phelps

Take control of your health

We're only granted one body.
Think about how we treat it.
Most of us take better care of our cars.
Take a positive, proactive view.
Learn about your health needs.
Give your body the food, the exercise
and the rest it deserves.
It will repay you and those who love you.

If anything is sacred the human body is sacred.
Walt Whitman

Clean up

No matter how long the mess has been there.
No matter how powerful the urge is to leave it there.
Make the effort to clean it up.
It's worth it.
It opens up new horizons.
It brings freshness.
It opens up new perspectives.

Our life is frittered away with detail … Simplify, simplify.
Henry David Thoreau

It's never too late to …

Say no

No sounds so simple,
but many people find it almost impossible to say.
They lack the confidence.
They fear giving offence.
But when you know it's right –
when you know you'll regret it if you don't say it –
have courage.
Say no.
Other options will arise.
Others will respect you.

Which part of 'no' don't you understand?
Anonymous

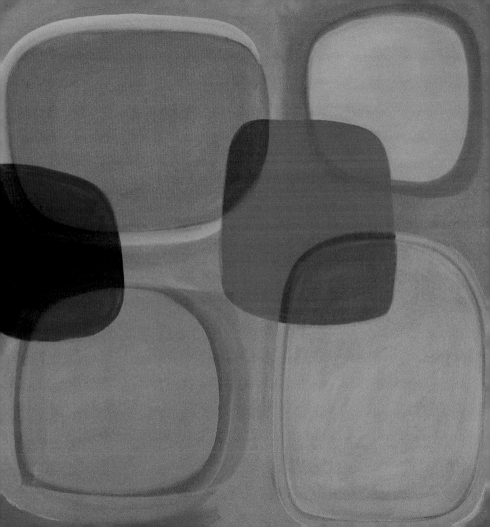

Prioritise

It's worth the time and the effort.
Consider the options before you.
Mull over the relative importance of
your tasks and duties.
Assign weight to each one.
Attack them in order of importance.
You'll be stunned at how that will free you up.
And how many seemingly pressing things
fade into insignificance.

A pint of sweat will save a gallon of blood.
General George S. Patton

Slow down

We miss so much as we rush headlong through life.
Take the time to observe.
Allow yourself to weigh options.
Listen to alternatives.
Deliberate over decisions.
Focus your energy on one thing at a time.
Widen your vision.

Everything that happens to you is your teacher. The secret is
to sit at the feet of your own life and be taught by it.
Mahatma Gandhi

Have a luxurious bath

When the stress is getting to you.
When you're tied up in knots.
Take time out.
Fill a warm bath.
Throw in the bath salts.
Close the door.
Turn out the lights.
Go on a mini retreat.
Embrace the silence, the solitude
and the gentle warmth.
Emerge with your batteries recharged.

Too much of a good thing is wonderful.
Armistead Maupin

Look up an old friend

It can be a sobering reality check.
Or a warm journey back in time.
Either way it is a journey worth taking.
Old friends act as measuring sticks.
They strip away the trimmings and layers of your life.
They are a mirror to your soul.

A friend is a present you give yourself.
Robert Louis Stevenson

Trace your family tree

It's a fascinating exercise.
It gives a feeling of continuity.
It answers many questions.
And poses many more.
Show your heritage.
Reveal your tribe.
Draw the world closer together.

If the past cannot teach the present and the father cannot
teach the son, then history need not have bothered to go on
and the world has wasted a great deal of time.
Russell Hoban

Master a new craft

Open yourself to new horizons.
Explore the potential of your skills
and your artistic abilities.
Find the right challenge.
It will bring satisfaction and joy.

We must use time as a tool not as a couch.
John Fitzgerald Kennedy

Focus

It's so easy to dissipate our energies –
to dilute our creativity on too many tasks at once.
Virtuosos apply all their skill and energy
to one aim at a time.
Select your key tasks.
Concentrate on one at a time.
Avoid distractions.
Marshall your skills.
Direct all your energies at your target.

Things which matter most must never be at
the mercy of things that matter least.
Johann Wolfgang von Goethe

Greet the sun

Rise before dawn.
Find a vantage point with a wide vista.
Wait for the first warming rays.
Feel their strength, their vitality.
Observe the world as it wakes around you.
Feel the renewal.

One touch of nature makes the whole world kin.
William Shakespeare

Give something back

Most of us spend a lot of time taking.
Whenever you can, take time to give back.
Whether it's love, or knowledge, power or money.
Take the opportunity.
It allows you to grow.
It enriches the lives of others.
The rewards are often intangible but they are great.

The quality of mercy is not strained … it is twice blessed;
it blesseth him that gives and him that takes.
William Shakespeare

Start a diary

Make your personal record,
your unique view of the world.
Keep it secure.
Write from your heart,
with passion, without fear.
It brings perspective.
It diminishes anger.
It allows reflection.

The mind is its own place. In itself it can make a
heaven of hell, and a hell out of heaven.
John Milton

Get political

When your passions are storming.
When your inner beliefs are aggrieved.
When you can no longer sit passively and watch.
Take a stand.
Get logical and try to make changes.
Figure out the politics and the power balances.
Then act with decisiveness and persistence.

The one thing that doesn't abide by majority rule
is a person's conscience.
Harper Lee

Think global

Many of our problems start locally but spread globally.
If you believe strongly enough,
you can make a difference.
Widen your vision.
With today's communications, the world is a village.
Start small: one on one.
Then with passion and purpose, spread your word.
There are no boundaries.

Your playing small doesn't serve the world.
Marianne Williamson